"Hey! Wait for me!"

"This is the Place!"

Sputnik and the Mutant Ants from Mars

Someone lost his toy.

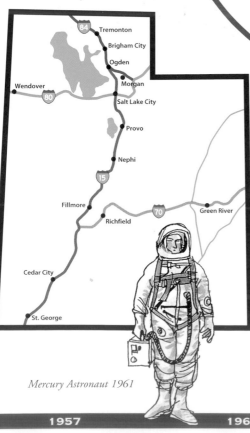

Map: Utah Freeways
The Interstate Highway System was authorized in 1956 to create a nationwide transportation system to move troops and equipment quickly in the event of war. The first freeways came to Utah in the 1950s.

Tremonton
Brigham City
Ogden
Wendover
Morgan
Salt Lake City
Provo
Nephi
Fillmore
Green River
Richfield
Cedar City
St. George

Mercury Astronaut 1961

Atomic Rocket
Space toys with a nuclear theme were popular in the 1950s. The "Atomic Rocket" was made in Japan, 1955 and it was made of tin.

2/3 actual size

Seven-year-old Anthony Dunn played in the backyard. Sometimes he was Davy Crockett, sometimes Space Ranger Dan. At the moment he was fighting grizzly bears on Mars.

The sound of the radio drifted from the house. He liked television better–Dad had just bought one–but nothing much was on in the daytime.

Suddenly the music stopped and a man's voice came on the radio. "We interrupt to bring you this special bulletin: A Soviet rocket has put a satellite called *Sputnik* into orbit around the earth. The Soviet Politburo called it a victory for Communism . . ."

Anthony peered up at the sky. He didn't see any rocket. But the man on the radio sounded excited. Maybe the Communists will drop bombs from up there, Anthony thought. Maybe they will drop bombs on me and I will turn into a giant radioactive ant like the ones in that movie that my brother Alec saw. Anthony rushed into the house, forgetting the toy rocket he'd crashed deep into a make-believe Mars.

World News 1957
Dr. Suess publishes *The Cat in the Hat* • President Dwight David Eisenhower (known as "Ike") desegregates Arkansas schools • Brooklyn Dodgers move to Los Angeles • New York Giants move to San Francisco • Common Market founded in Europe • Britain detonates thermonuclear weapon • International Atomic Energy Commission established • Khrushchev rises to power in Soviet Union • Mao Tse-tung consolidates power in China • Egypt nationalizes the Suez Canal • Donny Osmond and Eddie Van Halen born

History
The United States and the Soviet Union became rivals for influence and prestige after the defeat of Nazi Germany in WWII. This conflict was called the Cold War.

On October 4, 1957, the Soviet Union shocked the world when they launched *Sputnik*, the first artificial satellite, into orbit around the earth. America saw this as a challenge to its technological leadership and embarked on a massive program of its own. The space race had begun.

Companies with facilities in Utah played a significant role in this contest. Sperry, Thiokol Chemical Corporation, and Hercules were involved in missile technology even before *Sputnik* circled the earth, and Thiokol continues to make the booster rockets that put American shuttles into space.

SPACE

1957 | 1960 | 1965 | 1970

October 1957 *Sputnik I* orbits Earth | January 1958 United States launches *Explorer I* | October 1959 Soviet *Luna 3* reaches and photographs moon | April 1961 Soviet Yuri Gagarin first man in space | May 1961 Alan Shepard first American in space | June 1965 Astronaut Edward White walks in space | 1966 Soviet *Luna 9* and U.S. *Surveyor 1* land on moon | December 1968 *Apollo 8* orbits moon | July 1969 Neil Armstrong walks on moon | April 1970 *Apollo 13* avoids disaster | December 1972 *Apollo 17*—last manned trip to moon | May 1973 *Skylab* U.S. space station launched

5 7

Pink Floyd

In the '50s plastic flamingos were popular lawn ornaments. The Great Salt Lake got its own "ornament" when a Chilean flamingo escaped from Salt Lake's Tracy Aviary in 1988. Dubbed "Pink Floyd" it took up residence in the lake not far from the Saltair resort. Floyd was last seen in 1991.

Shasta

With a tiger mother and lion father, Shasta was the first "liger" in the United States. Born in 1948 at Salt Lake's Hogle Zoo, she remained a popular attraction until her death in 1972. Shasta was stuffed and mounted and can still be seen on display with the other big cats at Hogle Zoo.

Believe it or don't!

■ Utahns eat more ice cream than anyone else in America. Utah produces 9,375,000 gallons of ice cream per year and each Utahn consumes 8.4 gallons—the highest average in the nation and more than twice the national average of 4 gallons per person.

■ President Dwight David Eisenhower had Utah's Snelgrove ice cream flown in for a White House Thanksgiving dinner.

■ Between 1953 and 1963 the U.S. government conducted more than 200 aboveground nuclear tests in the Nevada desert. Prevailing winds carried radioactive fallout from the tests to St. George and Utah's Dixie.

■ The first Harman's Kentucky Fried Chicken in America opened in 1954 on State Street in Salt Lake City.

■ A piece of moon rock brought back by Apollo astronauts is on display at the University of Utah's Museum of Natural History.

■ In October 1957, for the first time in LDS church history, a semi-annual general conference was cancelled due to a flu outbreak.

Lake Level

In 1963, the Great Salt Lake hits historic low at 4,191.3 feet above sea level.

UTAH BY THE NUMBERS

Number of Miss Americas from Utah: 2

Number of speed records set by Ab Jenkins in 1950 on Bonneville Salt Flats: 26

Age of Ab Jenkins in 1950: 67

Top speed achieved by Ab Jenkins in his 1950 record-setting drive: 199 mph

Record time it took Ab Jenkins to drive from New York to San Francisco in 1926: 86 hrs 20 min

Land speed record set 1970 by Gary Gabelich on the Bonneville Salt Flats: 622 mph

If the Great Salt Lake received no inflow of water, number of years it would take to evaporate: 4

Record time Marine aviator John Glenn took to fly from California to New York in 1957: 3 hrs 24 min

Number of years from white settlement until population reached one million: 118

Number of years to reach second million at current growth rate: 35

Utah Population: 1960—890,627.

Indian population 1960—6,961.
Utah reached 1,000,000 in 1964, 1965, or 1966—depending on who you believe. The *Ogden Standard Examiner* said Utah passed the mark in January 1964. State authorities claimed it happened on September 24, 1965, but the Bureau of Census said the state was still 10,000 shy of the big mark.

Philo T. Farnsworth

The inventor of television was born in 1906 in a log cabin at Indian Creek, near Beaver. At the age of 15, Philo figured out how to transmit pictures electronically with an "image dissector," and in 1927, he transmitted and received the first television picture. He also helped invent baby incubators and the electron microscope before he died in 1971. He hardly ever watched TV himself.

Mormon Meteor III

Racer David Abbott (Ab) Jenkins set a number of speed and endurance records on Utah's Bonneville Salt Flats in Mormon Meteor III—a car he built. He served as mayor of Salt Lake City from 1940 to 1943. The Mormon Meteor III is on permanent display at the State Capitol in Salt Lake City.

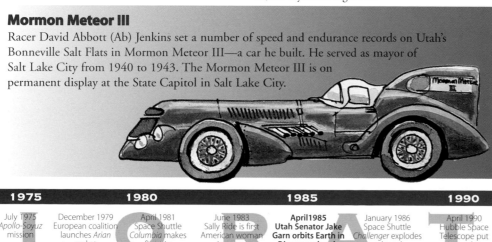

P L O R A T I O N

1975	1980		1985	1990		1995
July 1975 *Apollo-Soyuz* mission	December 1979 European coalition launches *Arian* rocket	April 1981 Space Shuttle *Columbia* makes first trip	June 1983 Sally Ride is first American woman in space	January 1986 Space Shuttle *Challenger* explodes on launch	April 1990 Hubble Space Telescope put into orbit	December 1993 Hubble Space Telescope repaired
			April1985 Utah Senator Jake Garn orbits Earth in *Discovery* shuttle			**September 1995 Space Shuttle *Discovery* visits SLC**

The Price of Liberty

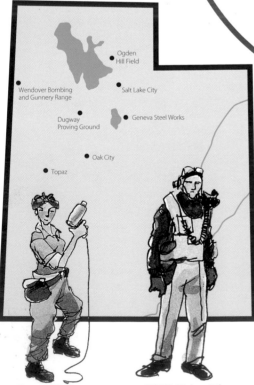

Wings!

Martha sat on the bench with her husband, Jack. On her lap was a small box that had just arrived in the mail. She carefully opened it. Inside were medals, coins, pens, photos, and a stack of letters tied with a red ribbon. She picked up a photo that showed Martha and Jack with their son, Grant, in his army uniform. He wore his hat at a rakish angle, trying to look older than his twenty years. Martha picked up the bundled letters. She already knew what they said—she had written them all. Her last letter was unopened. It had arrived at Grant's squadron the day after his fighter was shot down. A month ago a telegram from the War Department told them that their son was missing and presumed dead. A letter followed from Grant's commander: their son's plane had gone down in flames. His squadron saw no parachute. Fellow airmen had sent his personal effects in the box that was now on Martha's lap. She stared at her unopened letter without really seeing it.

Then she quietly began to cry, the box slipping off her lap and spilling on the ground. Jack gathered her in his arms and whispered what comfort he could before he too was unable to speak through his tears.

Later Jack picked up the contents of the box. He missed the pilot's wings.

actual size

U. S. Army Air Corps Pilot's Wings
The Air Force was a branch of the Army in World War II. The U.S. Army Air Corps became the U.S. Air Force in 1948.

Map: Utah in World War II
Utah was the site of military bases, industrial installations, prisoner-of-war camps, and detention camps during World War II.

- Ogden
  Hill Field
- Wendover Bombing and Gunnery Range
- Salt Lake City
- Dugway Proving Ground
- Geneva Steel Works
- Oak City
- Topaz

Factory Worker   *WWII Fighter Pilot*

World News 1945
FDR dies at Warm Springs, Georgia, April 14
• Harry S. Truman becomes president • Adolf Hitler commits suicide in Berlin, April 30
• Germany surrenders May 7 and is divided into four parts administered by the American, British, French, and Soviet militaries • Truman, Churchill, and Stalin meet at Potsdam in July
• U.S. drops the atomic bomb on Hiroshima, Japan, August 6 • A second atomic bomb is dropped on Nagasaki, August 9 • Japan surrenders August 14 • General George S. Patton killed in a car wreck • B-25 bomber flies into Empire State Building • United Nations organized in San Francisco

History
Before World War II, a global economic crisis called the Great Depression put tens of millions of people out of work and contributed to the rise of Hitler in Germany. In the United States, Utah was one of the states hit hardest. Unemployment was 36%, the fourth highest in the nation. But when the U.S. went to war against Germany and Japan in 1941, massive government spending started in Utah. Able-bodied Utahns, mostly young men, entered the armed services. Women filled in for absent men in factories and offices across the state.

One out of every two Utah families had someone in the armed forces, so most Utahns celebrated the end of the war and news that loved ones would be back. Others celebrated knowing that sons, husbands, and fathers had made victory possible but wouldn't be coming home.

| 1945 | 1950 | 1955 | 1960 | 1965 |

C   G   O   L   D

1945 End of WWII; Atomic bomb; U.N. founded • 1946 "Iron Curtain" across Eastern Europe • 1948 Soviets start Berlin blockade; Israel founded • 1949 Soviets test atomic bomb • 1950 Korean War; Senator Joe McCarthy starts "witch hunts" • 1952 America tests the hydrogen bomb • 1953 Stalin dies; USSR detonates hydrogen bomb • 1956 Soviets crush Hungarian revolt • 1959 Cuban revolution; Fidel Castro • 1961 Berlin Wall built • 1962 Cuban Missile Crisis • 1964 Gulf of Tonkin Resolution; Vietnam War • 1967 Israel "Six Day War" • 1968 Soviets invade Czechoslovakia

45

The Peregrine Falcon

Decimated by pesticides in the 1950s, the endangered peregrine falcon is making a comeback in its home range of Utah. A nesting pair traditionally make their summer home on the Joseph Smith Memorial Building (formerly the Hotel Utah) in downtown Salt Lake City.

The Mule Deer

Native to Utah, the mule deer is a favorite game animal. Male mule deer are rated according to the size of their "rack," or antlers. Utah's largest mule deer was taken in San Juan county and is the seventh largest in the world.

Believe it or don't!

■ One of the beaches stormed by American forces in the D-Day invasion of Normandy was code-named "Utah."

■ Harvey Natchees, a highly decorated Ute from Altonah, Utah, was the first U.S. serviceman to enter Berlin in 1945.

■ The army considered Oak City, Utah, as a site for the super-secret "Manhattan Project" to develop the atomic bomb before deciding on Los Alamos in New Mexico.

■ The B-29 crew that dropped the first atomic bomb on Japan secretly trained for the mission in Wendover, Utah. The "dummy" nuclear bombs they dropped on the West Desert are still there.

■ The government built Geneva Steel Works in Utah Valley at a cost of $200 million in 1943.

■ 8,000 Japanese-Americans spent the war in the Topaz detention camp in Utah's West Desert. On arriving, one girl looked at her desolate surroundings and wondered when she could go back to America. Years later the U.S. government apologized for imprisoning these loyal Americans.

Lake Level
The lake level is very low at 4,197 feet above sea level.

UTAHNS AT WAR

Spanish American War	Volunteered : 700 Died : 9
World War I	Served : 24,500 Died: 665
World War II	Served : 70,000 Died : 1,450
Korean War	Served: 7,564 Died : 436
Vietnam	Served: 47,000 Died: 369 men and 1 woman
	Missing in Action: 19

UTAH BY THE NUMBERS

Age of youngest Utahn killed in World War I: 15

Number of Utahns to receive Congressional Medal of Honor: 6

Diving speed of the peregrine falcon: 220 mph

Deer taken in 1945 deer hunt by 72,000 hunters: 50,000

Deer taken in 1995 deer hunt by 97,000 hunters: 27,306

Cost of first Utah deer license in 1907: $1

Cost of Utah deer license in 1995: $30

Current deer population in Utah: 400,000

Utah Population: 590,000.
Indian population 1950: 4,201.

Two Utahns won the Congressional Medal of Honor in WWII for heroism which cost them their lives:

Captain Mervyn S. Bennion
Died on Dec. 7, 1941, at Pearl Harbor. His actions as captain of the U.S.S. *West Virginia* during the Japanese surprise attack saved many lives.

Pfc. Jose F. Valdez
In January 1945 he held off 200 German troops, allowing his unit to escape. Valdez was mortally wounded and died after crawling back to his own lines.

U.S.S. *Utah*

The battleship U.S.S. *Utah* was commissioned in August 1911 and during World War I served in the Irish Sea. She was sunk on December 7, 1941, at Pearl Harbor with the loss of 58 men. The wreck of the *Utah* is part of the Pearl Harbor Memorial. The ship's bell can be seen in front of the Naval Science building at the University of Utah.

1975   1980   1985   1990   1995

W A R

1972 Nixon visits China; "Détente" with USSR

1975 Vietnam—Communist victory

1979 Soviets invade Afghanistan

1982 Leonid Brezhnev dies

1983 Reagan calls USSR "evil empire"

1985 Mikhail Gorbachev starts "glasnost"

1987 Chernobyl nuclear disaster

1989 Berlin Wall falls

1991 USSR collapses

1993 Fidel Castro encourages capitalist investment in Cuba

The Epidemic

Look at this neat bottle... I wonder what was in it...?

It was cold, but Alice Debenham's forehead glistened with sweat. The hot, humid feel of the upstairs room clung to her as she stepped outside. She breathed to clear her head. The sky was just turning pink with the rising sun. Sooty fog blanketed the valley below.

Her best friend's little Rachel had died, as had Jane Walker's husband, Hyrum, the very picture of health. He had taken ill and died in less than a week. Only 1 in 50 who got the Spanish flu died, but it seemed much worse than that. She'd lost count of people she knew who had come down with the fever, delirium, and racking cough that often turned deadly. Alice's two children and husband showed the first symptoms three days before.

It had been a nightmare of fevers, dirty linen, camphors, castor oil, herbal teas, and urgent prayers. Then Alice's grandmother brought by a homemade remedy. She said the stuff in the little blue medicine bottle was used by her grandmother. Maybe it helped, maybe it didn't, but the fevers had broken and her children and husband would live.

Morning light touched the mountains across the valley. The empty bottle slipped from Alice's fingers.

Medicine Bottle
Cobalt blue bottles were popularly used for keeping medicine. The dark glass prevented light from denaturing the contents.

actual size

History

November 1918 was a memorable month for Utahns. World War I ended on the 11th when Germany surrendered. On the 19th, LDS church president Joseph F. Smith died from a lingering illness, and Heber J. Grant became head of the Church. But the event which most directly touched the lives of Utahns was the influenza epidemic.

The misnamed Spanish flu started in the Far East and swept the world, killing millions. It reached Utah in early October. Measures were taken to stop the flu's spread. Schools and businesses closed, people wore gauze masks in public, and others lived in tents, believing fresh air helped. Some towns isolated themselves to prevent infection. Despite these actions a number of towns were especially hard hit. Tremonton, Brigham City, Wendover, and Henefer suffered unusually high mortality rates. Salt Lake City and Ogden each had 300 deaths. Statewide, 1,500 people died.

There still is no cure for the flu, but the recommended treatment in 1918 is still the prescription today—rest and fluids.

Map: National Parks and Monuments in Utah

What's the difference between a National Park and a National Monument? Presidents can authorize monuments, but Congress must approve parks.

Turn-of-the-century nurse

WWI U.S. Infantry "Doughboy"

Golden Spike National Historical Site
Flaming Gorge National Recreation Area
Timpanogos Cave National Monument
Dinosaur National Monument
Arches National Park
Capitol Reef National Park
Canyonlands National Parks
Cedar Breaks National Monument
Bryce Canyon National Park
Natural Bridges National Monument
Glen Canyon National Recreation Area
Hovenweep National Monument
Zion National Park
Rainbow Bridge National Monument

World News

Germany surrenders November 11, 1918—the eleventh hour of the eleventh day of the eleventh month • Woodrow Wilson leads U.S. through World War I and the Versailles Peace Conference • League of Nations founded (the U.S. never joined) • European empires, weakened by the war, are in their last days • Czar Nicholas II and his family murdered by the Bolsheviks holding them in Russia • Soviet government supports a worldwide communist movement • Daylight saving time and airmail postage introduced.

1900 · 1910 · 1920 · 1930 · 1940

1885 Louis Pasteur proposes germ theory of infection

1895 X-rays discovered

1899 Aspirin developed

1908 Concept of allergies introduced

1910 Marie Curie describes radioactivity

1912 Kasimir Funks invents the word *vitamine*

1922 Insulin treatment for diabetics developed

1923 Diphtheria vaccine developed

1928 Alexander Fleming discovers penicillin

1930 Vaccine for yellow fever introduced

1935 Discovery of sulfa drug for infections

1940 Howard Florey develops penicillin as a practical antibiotic

1942 U of U College of Medicine expands from two- to four-year program

The lobelia used today as an ornamental border in flower gardens is related to a favorite Pioneer medicinal herb, but the plant is also highly toxic with unpleasant side effects. Pioneer doctor and Mormon church leader Willard Richards's favorite remedy for most anything was lobelia and cayenne.

Old Ephraim

The last grizzly bear in Utah was shot in 1923 by a shepherd tired of losing his sheep. "Old Ephraim" weighed 1,000 pounds. His grave can still be seen in Logan Canyon.

Lake Level
The lake level is average at 4,203 feet above sea level.

Believe it or don't!

■ Air quality was awful in turn-of-the-century Utah. Homes and businesses burned coal, which fouled the air. In 1919 officials targeted the "smoke nuisance" and by 1921 the situation had improved.

■ In 1905, Murray farmers filed the first environmental lawsuit in the United States against smelters whose smoke was poisoning their cows and crops. The farmers won the case.

■ In 1916, Simon Bamberger, founder of Lagoon, was elected governor, becoming the second Jewish governor in America.

■ Most doctors in Utah in the 1800s were women.

■ Provo passed a "flu ordinance" during the Spanish flu outbreak; anyone caught in public without a gauze mask could be tossed in jail or fined $50.

■ Zion National Park was originally established as Mukuntuweap National Monument in 1909. The name was changed in 1918 to Zion National Monument and it became Zion National Park in 1919.

■ St. Marks in Salt Lake was the first hospital west of the Mississippi.

■ At the news that Germany had surrendered, a fight broke out among German prisoners of war held at Fort Douglas on Salt Lake's east bench. It was discovered they had been digging escape tunnels.

■ At the turn of the century, one in five infants died before its first birthday.

■ No public funeral was held for LDS church president Joseph F. Smith because of the flu epidemic.

■ The electric traffic light was invented by Salt Lake policeman Lester Wire in 1912.

UTAH BY THE NUMBERS

People killed in World War I: 10 million

People killed in 1918 Spanish flu epidemic: 20 million

Fatalities from deer mouse-borne Hanta virus outbreak in 1993: 50

Utahns killed by bears and cougars in last 150 years: 0

Percent of deer mice recently tested in the state found to carry the Hanta virus: 18

U.S. troops killed in combat in World War I: 34,000

U.S. troops killed by Spanish flu in 1918: 24,000

Utah soldiers killed in combat in World War I: 219

Utah soldiers killed by Spanish flu in 1918: 414

Utahns who wouldn't be alive today without modern medicine: 2 out of 3

Life expectancy in 1900: 49 years

Life expectancy today: 75 years

Utah Population: 440,000.
Indian population, 1920: 2,711.

The Deer Mouse
This otherwise harmless animal is responsible for the 1993 Hanta virus outbreak in the southwest U.S. The disease is often hard to detect because its symptoms mirror those of the flu, but it has an astonishing 50% mortality rate.

Doctor Ellis R. Shipp

This medical pioneer studied medicine in Philadelphia and gave birth to her sixth child while in her second year of studies. She graduated with high honors and returned to Utah where she helped deliver 5,000 babies over her fifty-year career and made tremendous contributions to the quality of health care in the state.

| 1950 | 1960 | 1970 | 1980 | 1990 | 2000 |

M E D I C I N E

- 1953 Lung cancer linked to cigarette smoking
- 1954 Jonas E. Salk develops anti-polio serum
- 1956 Oral vaccine for polio
- 1967 First heart transplant
- 1970 Khorana synthesizes a gene
- 1975 Physicians diagnose diseases before childbirth
- 1976 CAT scans introduced
- 1981 AIDS described as a disease
- 1982 Barney Clark receives first artificial heart in Salt Lake City
- 1993 Hanta virus outbreak in the U.S. Southwest

The 45th State

What's a medal doing here?

Gerald Morgan tugged on the reins and stopped to view the city below where thousands celebrated statehood. He thought back on the good luck that had brought him to this valley and made him one of the richest men in the territory—"state," he corrected himself.

He had left Ireland for America at fourteen and found work pounding spikes for the Transcontinental Railroad. The golden spike he'd seen driven home at Promontory Summit in 1869 meant two things: America now had a rail line spanning the continent and Gerald was out of work.

But he was in luck—he was in Utah. The Mormons viewed prospecting as disreputable, but a hard-working Catholic lad had no such qualms, and Gerald struck it rich. His luck held. He now owned a newspaper, two saloons, a hardware store, a stable, and the richest silver mine this side of Carson City.

He liked the view here. Perhaps a little country house away from his mansion in the city might be nice. From his pocket he pulled a commemorative statehood medal —probably made of silver from his mine. He deliberately tossed it to the frozen ground to mark the site of his future home—for luck.

World News 1896

William McKinley defeats William Jennings Bryan for U.S. presidency • Gold is discovered in the Klondike • Steven Crane publishes *The Red Badge of Courage* • New York theaters begin showing "flickers"—moving pictures • Southern Europeans—Greeks, Italians, Serbs—immigrate to Utah • First Alpine ski school established at Lilienfeld, Austria • Abyssinians defeat the Italians • Alfred Nobel, inventor of dynamite, dies. His will establishes the Nobel Prizes • First modern Olympics held in Athens, Greece • Queen Victoria celebrates her Diamond Jubilee

actual size

The Swaner Medal
This commemorative medal featuring the state seal was sold at the January 6, 1896, Statehood Day celebration in the LDS Tabernacle. (Note the date on Medal-Utah was actually admitted January 4)

History

The U.S. Congress denied Utah's first six applications for statehood over the issues of polygamy and LDS church control of local politics. It took fifty years and the abandonment of polygamy in 1890 to pave the way for statehood six years later.

But two events in the previous decades ensured that Mormon isolationism in their mountain stronghold would end and bring Utah into the American mainstream. U.S. soldiers stationed in Utah in the 1860s found precious metals, and an influx of non-Mormon prospectors, miners, and merchants followed. The second event was the completion of the Transcontinental Railroad in 1869. It tied Utah with iron bands to America's social and political life. The LDS church would continue to exert a significant influence on the state, but Utahns began to view themselves as Americans with loyalties to its institutions and traditions. President Grover Cleveland finally signed the law making Utah a state on January 4, 1896.

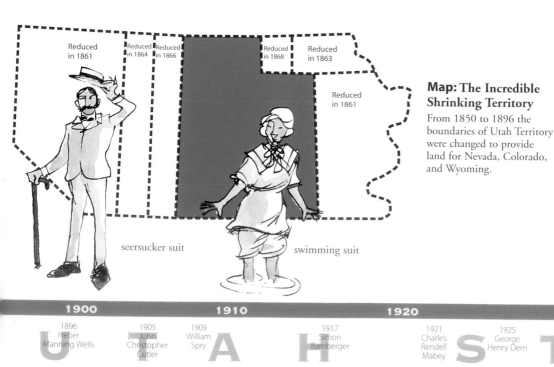

Reduced in 1861 | Reduced in 1864 | Reduced in 1866 | Reduced in 1868 | Reduced in 1863 | Reduced in 1861

Map: The Incredible Shrinking Territory
From 1850 to 1896 the boundaries of Utah Territory were changed to provide land for Nevada, Colorado, and Wyoming.

seersucker suit

swimming suit

1900   1910   1920   1930   1940

U T A H S T A T E

1896 Heber Manning Wells | 1905 John Christopher Cutler | 1909 William Spry | 1917 Simon Bamberger | 1921 Charles Rendell Mabey | 1925 George Henry Dern | 1933 Henry Hooper Blood | 1941 Herbert Brown Maw

96

Sego Lily
The sego lily became the official state flower on March 18, 1911, after a census of the state's schoolchildren to determine their preference. The sego lily grows six to eight inches tall. Indians and Pioneers ate the sego lily's bulbs, which are about the size of a walnut.

California Gull
The California gull became the state bird in 1933 in honor of its "insectivorous" appetite (it eats bugs—see Mormon crickets).

Beehive
The beehive shown on the Utah State Seal is a "skep." This type of beehive dates to Europe in the Middle Ages and is made of straw reinforced with clay.

Believe it or don't!
■ President Cleveland refused to allow a Utah delegation to witness the signing of the statehood declaration, saying it was just routine business. Only the president and his secretary, Mr. Thurber, were present.

■ Utah's statehood proclamation was signed on January 4, 1896, but the celebration took place two days later so it wouldn't fall on a Sunday.

■ Elected State officials were publicly sworn in at statehood ceremonies in Salt Lake's Mormon Tabernacle on Temple Square.

■ The door of the Tabernacle was smashed in and anxious crowds occupied the reserved seats to witness statehood ceremonies.

■ Utah women were given the vote in 1870—the second territory in the nation to give women this privilege.

■ Although he lost the presidential election in 1896, William Jennings Bryan received 82.7% of the popular vote in Utah.

Lake Level
The level of the Great Salt Lake is average at 4,202 feet above sea level.

UTAH BY THE NUMBERS
The high in Salt Lake the day Utah was made a state: 35°F

The low in Salt Lake the day Utah was made a state: 12°F

Of Utah's first four governors, number that were foreign born: 3

Number of cars in Utah in 1900: 20

Number of cars in Utah in 1996: 900,000 (not including 630,000 light trucks)

Number of years Fillmore was the territorial capital: 5

Number of people who jammed into the Tabernacle for statehood ceremonies: 15,000

Martha Maria Hughes Cannon
The polygamous wife of Angus Munn Cannon, she earned a medical degree from the University of Michigan at 23. In 1897 she defeated her husband to become the first female state senator in the U.S. *The Salt Lake Tribune* called her the best man for the job. She was the mother of three, a faithful Mormon, and an independent thinker who worked for women's rights. The Utah Department of Health building is named for her.

Utah Population: 250,000.
1890 census found 3,456 Indians living in Utah, but by 1900 the number had declined to 2,623.

The Blue Spruce
Utah legislators quickly approved the Utah Federation of Women's Club's bill to make the blue spruce Utah's state tree in 1933 when they learned that the Colorado legislature was considering making it Colorado's state tree.

Heber M. Wells
Utah's first governor was one of 36 children of LDS church official and former Salt Lake mayor Daniel H. Wells. He began his career as a tax collector. Wells was an accomplished actor and an excellent swimmer. Elected at 36, Wells remains the youngest person ever elected governor of Utah.

1950	1960	1970	1980	1990
1949 Joseph Bracken Lee	1957 George Dewey Clyde	1965 Calvin Lewellyn Rampton	1977 Scott Milne Matheson	1985 Norman Howard Bangerter

1993 Michael Leavitt

G O V E R N O R S

Polygamy on the Run

Pirate gold!

Porter Bennion looked to see if he'd been followed. Federal marshals had nearly nabbed him at his first wife's house, but a hiding place under the stairs saved him.

Traveling at twilight seemed prudent. His second wife, Olivia Martha Bradley Bennion, had a place in the city. Or perhaps he'd stay with her sister, his third wife, Penelope Bradley Bennion, in Centerville. Her neighbors were discreet and adhered devoutly to the Mormon motto: "Mind your own business." They wouldn't turn him in to the snooping marshals who were after "polygs" like himself. If they caught him . . .

He could just make out the territorial penitentiary in the distance. Many of his friends and fellow polygamists were there.

Polygamy might seem a little odd, but who was it hurting? He was a good husband and gave what support he could to his wives. It angered him to be persecuted by the government for living his deeply held religious beliefs. He strode away with renewed determination but without his lucky twenty-dollar Mormon gold coin. It had slipped out of a hole in his pocket.

World News 1885
Grover Cleveland inaugurated president • Victor Hugo, author of *The Hunchback of Notre Dame*, dies • Statue of Liberty arrives from France • Washington Monument completed • Johannes Brahms completes Fourth Symphony • Gottlieb Daimler invents the motorcycle • Congress outlaws barbed wire on public lands • In Sudan, the Mahdi seizes Khartoum and kills English General C. G. Gordon • Germany annexes Zanzibar and Tanganyika • Robert Louis Stevenson publishes *Dr. Jekyll and Mr. Hyde* • Dr. Pepper goes on sale in Texas • Philadelphian John M. Fox learns about golf on a vacation to Scotland and introduces it to America

Twice actual size

1849 Mormon Twenty-dollar Gold Piece
Brigham Young authorized the minting of gold coins to make up for the scarcity of hard cash in Utah. The coin above features a Phrygian three-pointed crown above the all-seeing eye. It is worth $45,000 today.

History
Mormon polygamy allowed a man to marry more than one woman. The practice was begun by the religion's founder, Joseph Smith, in the 1830s and remained an open secret until 1852 when the doctrine was made public in an LDS church general conference.

This set off a firestorm among Americans who considered polygamy immoral. Congress worked hard to outlaw the practice, and the newly organized Republican party pledged to end the "twin relics of barbarism—polygamy and slavery." In 1882 Congress passed the Edmunds Act, authorizing federal officials to imprison polygamists and strip the LDS church of its property. Many high-ranking Mormon leaders were imprisoned in the territorial penitentiary (the site of today's Sugar House Park), and Church president John Taylor died while hiding from federal officials. Polygamy ended in 1890 when the new prophet, Wilford Woodruff, stopped the practice in an official statement called "the Manifesto."

Imprisoned polygamists wore suits of prison "stripes."

Map: State of Deseret
In 1849 Brigham Young outlined borders for the "State of Deseret" that stretched from the Rocky Mountains to the beaches of Southern California.

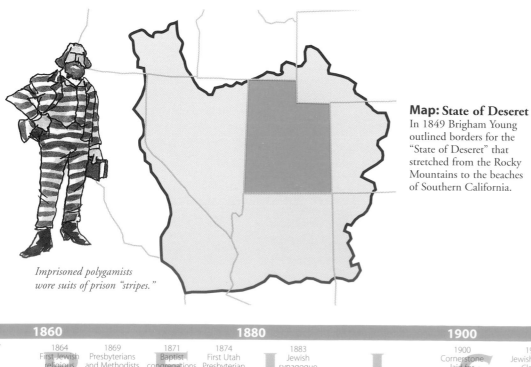

1860   **1880**   **1900**   **1920**

R E L I G I O N

1864 First Jewish religious service in Utah • 1869 Presbyterians and Methodists begin missionary work in Utah • 1871 Baptist congregations in Utah • 1874 First Utah Presbyterian Church established • 1883 Jewish synagogue built • 1900 Cornerstone laid for Cathedral of the Madeleine • 1910 Jewish city of Clarion established • 1912 Buddhist congregation established • 1917 Cathedral of the Madeleine dedicated • 1925 Holy Trinity Greek Orthodox Church consecrated

Sparrow

In 1877, 90 pairs of English sparrows were released in Salt Lake City to curb insect infestations. By 1888 the sparrows had multiplied and were themselves considered pests. A bounty of ¼ cent per bird was offered.

The Salt Lake Temple

Built of granite from a local canyon, the Salt Lake Temple was completed in 1893 after 40 years of construction.

Believe it or don't!

- "Mind Your Own Business" was popularly known as the Mormon Motto.
- George Leroy Parker, born in 1866 in Beaver, Utah, is better known as the outlaw Butch Cassidy.
- "Fundamentalist Mormon" describes those who still practice polygamy today in defiance of LDS church policy and state law.

Lake Level

After declining since the early 1870s, the Great Salt Lake began a rally that ended in 1885 at almost 4,208 feet above sea level.

UTAH BY THE NUMBERS

Number of wives generally credited to Brigham Young: 27

Number of Brigham Young's children: 56

Polygamists jailed in the 1880s: 1,200

Average time served by each convicted polygamist: 6 to 18 months

Number of "Fundamentalist" polygamists believed living in Utah today: 50,000

Number of Utahns who lost the right to vote in1882 with Edmunds-Tucker act: 12,000

Wall thickness at base of Salt Lake Temple: 12 feet

Height of Salt Lake Temple central spire: 220 feet

Number of lights used to decorate Temple Square at Christmas: 300,000

$800 REWARD!

JOHN TAYLOR GEORGE Q. CANNON

To be Paid for the Arrest of

JOHN TAYLOR,

President of the Mormon Church, and

George Q. Cannon,

His Counselor; or

$500 will be paid for Cannon alone, and $300 for Taylor.

Salt Lake City Jan 21, 1887.

Posters like these were circulated to aid in the capture of Mormon church leaders. The higher reward for Cannon was meant as an insult to President Taylor.

Utah Population: 175,000.
Indian: About 4,000.

John Taylor

The third president of the LDS church was born in 1808 in England. He joined the church in Canada in 1836. The mob that killed Joseph Smith also shot Taylor five times, and he became known as the Living Martyr. He led the church after Brigham Young's death when government persecution of Mormon polygamists was at its height. He died in 1887.

Samuel Clemens (aka Mark Twain)

In *Roughing It*, Twain recounts a visit to Salt Lake City where he meant to "reform" polygamy. But upon seeing the local women he wrote, "The man that marries one of them has done an act of Christian charity . . . and the man that marries sixty of them has done a deed of open-handed generosity so sublime that the nations should stand uncovered in his presence."

Mr. Clemens was just kidding.

1940   **1960**   **1980**

1930 LDS church celebrates centennial

1947 Mormon Pioneer centennial

1953 Polygamists jailed in raid on Short Creek

1970 David O. McKay dies

Hare Krishnas buy radio station in Utah valley

Cathedral of the Madeleine restoration

I N   U T A H

I've Been Working on the Railroad

It kinda looks like a nail.

Mike O'Malley and four friends made camp after dark, and in the morning were surprised to see the Chinese men making tea just a few feet from their campsite. Wong Sing and his cousins, all from Kwangtung Province, were equally surprised to find four hairy Irish barbarians from Cork as their neighbors. All the men were on their way to Park City, a new mining town, to find work.

The Irish laughed at the Chinese and their tea-and-rice breakfast, while the Chinese could hardly stand the smell of the salt pork and potatoes the Irishmen cooked over the campfire. The Irishmen were bitter over losing the track laying record. Wong could speak enough English to understand their insults, and he issued a challenge to O'Malley.

O'Malley and Wong set up two spikes in a log. Mike grabbed his spike-driving maul and drove a spike with four mighty strokes, completing the task in ten seconds. Then Wong Sing and Ka lined up on opposite sides of their spike, and with ten strokes drove home their spike—but they did it in only eight seconds. Once again, the Chinese had bested their Irish competition—and in the Irishmen's eyes, just as unfairly.

Iron Railroad Spike
Millions of these iron spikes were used to secure the rails to wooden ties to build the Transcontinental Railroad

actual size

Map: Transcontinental Railroad and mining districts

Miner

Promontory Summit

Transcontinental Railroad

Bingham Canyon
copper, gold, silver

Park City
silver and lead

Alta
silver

Stockton
copper, gold, silver

Ophir
lead, zinc, copper, gold, silver

Mercur *gold*

Frisco
silver, lead

Silver Reef
silver

Chinese and Irish railroad workers

World News 1869
Union general U.S. Grant sworn in as 18th president of the United States • John Wesley Powell leads first expedition down the Colorado River • First postcards sold in America • Number of U.S. Supreme Court judges increased from seven to nine • French Empress Eugenie opens Suez Canal • Mahatma Gandhi born in India • Jules Verne writes *20,000 Leagues under the Sea* about an imaginary submarine, the *Nautilus* • Women in Wyoming Territory are given the vote • French composer Hector Berlioz dies • Japanese emperor moves the capital from Kyoto to Tokyo • Princeton and Rutgers play first college football game in New Jersey • Cincinnati Red Stockings become first paid baseball team

History
In 1863, Congress authorized construction of a Transcontinental Railroad but work didn't really start until after the Civil War ended in 1865. In the East, the Union Pacific hired thousands of Irish emigrants, nicknamed "Paddies," while in the West, the Central Pacific hired 12,000 Chinese workers, known as "Celestials."

As both lines neared completion, a meeting spot was set at Promontory, Utah, north of the Great Salt Lake. Competition between the two railroad companies to see who could lay the most track was intense. The Central Pacific work gangs laid 10 miles of track between sunrise and sunset to set a record.

After the driving of the Golden Spike, on May 10, most of these workers were immediately unemployed. Many of the Chinese and Irish emigrants found work in the mining camps of Utah.

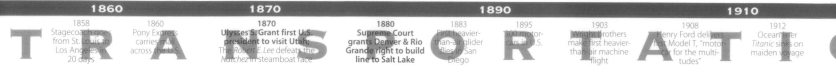

T R A N S C R I P T I O N

1860   1870   1890   1910

1858
Stagecoach goes from St. Louis to Los Angeles in 20 days

1860
Pony Express carries mail across the U.S.

1870
Ulysses S. Grant first U.S. president to visit Utah; The *Robert E. Lee* defeats the *Natchez* in steamboat race

1880
Supreme Court grants Denver & Rio Grande right to build line to Salt Lake

1883
First heavier-than-air glider flies in San Diego

1895
300 motor-cars in U.S.

1903
Wright Brothers make first heavier-than-air machine flight

1908
Henry Ford delivers first Model T, "motor car for the multitudes"

1912
Ocean liner *Titanic* sinks on maiden voyage

69

Silkworm

The Chinese might have been surprised to discover that the Mormons in Utah were trying to make silk. Brigham Young encouraged the development of home grown industry to make Utahns self-sufficient. Mulberry trees and silkworms were brought to Utah to start a silk industry. The enterprise had only limited success, but some of the mulberry trees remain.

Life in Utah

Since they lacked paved streets or sidewalks, Utah's cities were awash with mud when it rained. Horses sometimes sank up to their bellies in the muck.

Believe it or don't!

■ At Fossil Creek on May 28, 1869, Cheyennes destroyed a section of U.P. track and ransacked a train.

■ One of the worst massacres in U.S. history was committed by Col. Patrick Connor at the head of U.S. troops stationed in Utah. At the Battle of Bear River near Preston, Idaho, 250 Shoshoni men, women, and children were killed.

■ Fort Douglas on Salt Lake City's east bench was originally called Camp Douglas for Stephen A. Douglas, the man Lincoln defeated for the U.S. presidency in 1860.

■ Established in 1868, ZCMI (Zions Cooperative Mercantile Institution) was America's first department store.

■ The Pony Express first passed through Salt Lake City on April 7, 1860, at 11:45 P.M.

Lake Level

The level of the Great Salt Lake rose to its highest recorded point at 4,211 feet in 1869.

UTAH BY THE NUMBERS

Time for a transcontinental trip by wagon: 8 months

Time to deliver mail by Pony Express: 11 days

Time for a transcontinental trip by rail: 8 days

Miles of Class I rail lines in Utah: 1,420

U.S. railroad trackage in 1916: 254,251 miles

U.S. railroad trackage in 1986: 154,000 miles

Number of out-of-state visitors per year: 14 million

Income tourists generate: $2.9 billion

Utah Population: 86,000.
Indian population outside of reservations: 179.

Patrick Edward Connor

Connor was the commander of U.S. troops stationed in Utah during the Civil War. He had a great dislike of the Mormons, whom he called a "community of traitors, murderers [and] thieves" To Brigham Young's chagrin, he founded Camp Douglas in Salt Lake City and started an anti-Mormon newspaper. He encouraged his soldiers to prospect for gold and silver, hoping to create a gold rush that would swamp the Mormon inhabitants. He is known as the "Father of Utah Mining."

The Golden Spike

Brigham Young and most Utah dignitaries did not attend the ceremony to celebrate the driving of the last spike on the Transcontinental Railroad. They were annoyed that Salt Lake City had been bypassed in favor of Ogden. But thousands of railway dignitaries and employees were present as Leland Stanford of the Central Pacific symbolically joined the rails. He dropped a golden spike into a hole previously prepared for the occasion, then pulled it out and dropped another gold, a silver, and an alloyed spike (iron, silver, and gold), removing each in turn. The rails were finally joined by a common iron spike.

1925			1940		1948		1960		
1918	1928	1929	1937	1942	**1948**	1956	1958	1966	1986
Regular airmail service established between New York and Philadelphia	Ford produces last Model T, introduces Model A	Transcontinental Air Transport company opens coast-to-coast air service	Dirigible *Hindenburg* explodes while landing in New Jersey	Bell XP-59 flies; first American-built jet fighter planes	**First Utah oil well flows in Uintah County**	Interstate Highway System authorized	On a voyage of 1,880 miles, the First atomic submarine, U.S.S. *Nautilus* sails under North Pole	U.S. Department of Transportation established	Experimental plane *Voyager* circles the globe without refueling

Pioneer Tea Party

A toy spoon!

Johanna, Rebecca, and Eliza talked and laughed, enjoying their picnic. And they drank tea. Not real tea—that had run out long ago—but a bitter concoction made from Rocky Mountain herbs. Even so, the delicate china cups and silver spoons which had been brought West with such pains gave the drink a certain dignity.

They talked about their old homes in England, New York, and Pennsylvania. Eventually the talk died away and they gazed down at the distant adobe settlement—their new home.

Since arriving in the valley they'd worked as though their lives depended on it—which, in fact, they did. Americans had never settled the area before, and no one could say how bitter the coming winter might be. Somehow, they'd stolen a little time to have a picnic away from husbands, children, and the never-ending work. Not one of them dared guess when they'd get this chance again. So they lingered. When they realized the time, cups, spoons, pots, and quilts were hastily put up. It would be months before Eliza realized one of her silver teaspoons was gone.

Teaspoon
Made in England, 1828. Sterling silver.

actual size

World News 1847
James K. Polk is president • War with Mexico; U.S. forces capture Mexico City • Treaty of Guadalupe Hidalgo makes Utah part of the United States in 1848 • Charlotte Bronte publishes *Jane Eyre* • Inventors Alexander Graham Bell and Thomas Alva Edison born • American Medical Organization organized • U.S. government issues first adhesive postage stamps • Evaporated milk first produced • Liberia proclaimed an independent African republic • Composer Stephen Foster gets $100 for "Oh, Susannah"

History
The Latter-day Saints, or Mormons, were followers of Joseph Smith, who had been driven from homes in Missouri and Illinois. Following Smith's murder in 1844, Brigham Young led the Saints to Utah in 1847, seeking a refuge in the Rocky Mountains. Brigham Young was suffering from Rocky Mountain fever when the first Pioneer company entered the valley on July 22, but he was remembered years later as looking out over the valley and saying, "This is the right place. Drive on."

The first Pioneer company was made up of 143 men—including 3 African-Americans—3 women, 2 children, and 72 wagons. Two other companies arrived before winter. The Pioneers created a home in the wilderness, beginning with a fort built of adobes, or mud bricks, where Pioneer Park in Salt Lake now stands.

Map: The Mormon Trail
From 1847 to 1869 more than 60,000 Latter-day Saints crossed the plains on the Mormon Trail.

Pioneer women often drove wagon teams

Believe it or don't!

■ In 1846, the Donner party opened the road into the Salt Lake Valley that the Mormon Pioneer company later followed into Salt Lake.

■ The Salt Lake Valley was hardly a desert. It was lush and green with grass so tall that early Pioneers sometimes lost their cows and horses in it.

■ The first white child born in Utah, Elizabeth Young Steele, was born August 9, 1847.

■ The first Mormon to die in the Salt Lake Valley was three-year-old Milton Howard Threlkeld, who drowned in City Creek on August 11, 1847.

■ The University of Deseret (later the University of Utah) was established in 1850. It is the oldest American university west of the Missouri.

■ Three out of five deaths in early Utah were children under five years old.

Lake Level

When the Pioneers arrived, the lake level was lower than average. Explorer John C. Frémont rode his horse to Antelope Island in 1845. Captain Howard Stansbury made the first scientific measurement of the lake level in 1850. It was 4,201 feet above sea level.

Honeybee

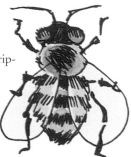

According to Mormon scripture, ancient Americans called the honeybee "deseret." The bee became the state insect due to the lobbying efforts of the fifth-grade class of Ridgecrest Elementary School. Governor Scott Matheson signed the honey bee law on March 16, 1983.

The Mormon Cricket

The Mormon cricket, *anabrus simplex,* is actually a grasshopper, though the Pioneers said it was a cross between a spider and a buffalo. The seagulls weren't the only ones to feast on crickets—the Indians taught the Mormon Pioneers how to mash roasted crickets and bake them into bread.

UTAH BY THE NUMBERS

Number of Pioneers who died at Winter Quarters in winter of 1846-47: 600

White population of Utah at the beginning of 1847: 12

White population of Utah at the end of 1847: 1,670

Number of towns established by Brigham Young: 325

Percent of 1847 pioneers under the age of twenty: 50%

Number of "prairie wolves" (probably coyotes) killed by Pioneers their first winter: 300

Age of Brigham Young when he entered Salt Lake Valley: 46

Utah Population: 2,000 whites. Indain population: About 25,000.

Brigham Young

Called the American Moses for leading the Mormons in an exodus to a new home in the mountains. His genius as an organizer and colonizer is stamped on the tidy communities that successfully settled the Great Basin. He died in 1877 at the age of 76.

Bulletin of the Plains

Pioneers left messages written on buffalo skulls for wagon companies that would come later.

Varmint Hunts

On Christmas 1848 the Pioneers organized a "varmint hunt" to kill "wasters and destroyers." Included were "wolves, wildcats, catamounts, pole cats, minks, bear, panthers, eagles, hawks, owls, ravens and magpies."

0	1925			1950		1975	2000
1911 LDS church adopts Boy Scout program	1924 First radio broadcast of general conference	1929 KSL begins broadcasting Mormon Tabernacle Choir	1936 LDS church welfare program initiated	1949 First general conference TV broadcast	1965 Family Home Evening program begun	1978 Priesthood given to all worthy males	LDS church membership approaches 10 million

Beads
Beads
Beads...

While their Indian wives set up camp, the mountain men argued about who discovered the Great Salt Lake.

The American said Jim Bridger discovered the lake in 1824. They could ask him themselves at the rendezvous.

"Balderdash!" said English Jack. An Englishman named Lawrence saw the lake back in 1790 on his way to California.

Manuel Garcia from New Mexico said it was his great-uncle Juan who came in 1776 with Fathers Dominguez and Escalante. Juan came back to trade and found the lake.

Jules du Bois, a Frenchman from Canada, said no, his uncle Martin LeCarne first saw the lake in 1760. Jules could show them where Martin had carved his name in a cave by the lake. And the next man to see the lake was also French— Etienne Provost.

The wives listened to this hubbub. Little Moon said they were all wrong. An eagle led the Ancient Ones to the lake so many moons ago that no one could count them all.

To settle the matter, English Jack took a swing at Jules. A patch of fancy beadwork went flying and disappeared in the grass.

Map: Exploring Utah

- - - - Dominguez-Escalante–1776

- - - - Jedediah Smith–1826-1827

actual size

Trade Beads
Indians made beads from dyed porcupine quills, but the colorful glass and ceramic beads from Europe were immensely popular among mountain men and Indians.

Early nineteenth-century mountain man

World News 1827
John Quincy Adams is president • John Dalton proposes his atomic theory • Mardi Gras celebrated for the first time in New Orleans • *Last of the Mohicans* is published in 1826 • Industrial revolution—railroads and steamboats • England outlaws slavery • Revolution in Mexico and South America • Power of Turkish Empire broken at Battle of Navarino when the English, French, and Russian fleets destroy the Turkish and Egyptian navies • Beethoven dies • John James Audubon publishes *Birds of North America* • John Walker introduces sulfur matches.

History
No one knows when the first European saw the Great Salt Lake. Fathers Dominguez and Escalante led an expedition that visited Utah Valley in 1776, but they turned south before reaching the lake. In 1824 Jim Bridger became the first white man of record to see the Great Salt Lake. He tasted its briny waters and thought he'd found the Pacific Ocean.

Trappers were quick to follow explorers into Utah. By the 1820s Americans from St. Louis, British traders from the Pacific Northwest, and Mexicans from Santa Fé were engaged in a fierce conflict over control of the rich trade in beaver pelts. Much of the battle took place in Utah.

American trappers met every summer at a *rendezvous* to trade furs for supplies brought in on pack trains. This let the trappers spend the entire year in the mountains, and many of them married Indian women and adopted their ways. They called themselves mountaineers–we remember them as mountain men.

1775	1800	1825	1850	18

1776
Dominguez and Escalante reach Utah

1779
Vitas Bering explores Arctic Ocean; Captain James Cook dies in Hawaii

1804
Lewis & Clark leave St. Louis for the Pacific; Zebulon Pike explores Colorado

1825
Peter Skene Ogden explores northern Utah

1827
Jedediah Smith goes from Great Salt Lake to the Pacific

1843
John C. Frémont explores the Great Salt Lake

1849
Parley P. Pratt explores Southern Utah; Stansbury surveys the Great Salt Lake

1853
John Gunnison killed on Sevier River exploring railroad route

1869
John Wesley Powell descends the Green and Colorado Rivers

Quaking Aspen

Stands of this delicate looking tree are found in higher elevations. The bark of quaking aspen is a beaver delicacy, and its heart-shaped leaves turn a vibrant yellow in the fall.

Mountain Buffalo

The Great Basin was once home to a bison that early explorers called mountain buffalo. Smaller and, according to mountain men, tastier than the buffalo of the Great Plains, the last mountain buffalo disappeared from Utah in the 1820s.

Believe it or don't!

■ The first American to settle in Utah was mountain man Miles Goodyear, who built a fort on the Weber River in 1846 and married an Indian woman named Pomona. Goodyear's cabin and reconstructed fort can be seen in Ogden.

■ Beavers were saved from extinction by a fashion whim–when silk top hats became popular in the 1840s, the beaver market collapsed.

■ In 1825 British and American trappers came close to bloodshed over which nation owned Weber Canyon. They were actually in Mexican territory.

■ John C. Frémont used an inflatable rubber boat to explore the Great Salt Lake in 1843.

■ Mulatto mountaineer Jim Beckwith wrote a popular book about his experiences, which included becoming a chief of the Crow tribe.

■ A cross carved in 1843 by Kit Carson on Frémont Island's Castle Rock can still be seen.

Lake Level

The lake was very high in 1826 when mountaineers James Clyman, Louis Vasquez, Henry G. Fraeb, and Moses "Black" Harris "floated around it" in a bull boat.

UTAH BY THE NUMBERS

Number of "Mountaineers" who worked the American fur trade: 2,000

Beavers killed to supply pelts for top hats: 2,000,000

Number of beavers in Utah today: 35,000

Price paid by collectors for an authentic trade bead from early 1800s: $100–$400

The Beaver Hat

In the early 1800s, the gentleman's top hat was made from beaver pelts.

The Beaver

Native to Utah's rivers and streams, the beaver was almost exterminated by the fur trade. In the years since, beavers have flourished and reestablished themselves in most of their old habitats. A full-grown beaver weighs between thirty and sixty pounds.

Jedediah Smith

In the 1820s Smith engaged in the first major explorations of Utah and was the first man to cross the continent to California. He grew his hair long to disguise a mangled ear suffered in a grizzly bear attack. He wrote, "I had traveled so much in the vicinity of the Salt Lake that it had become my home in the wilderness."

75   1900   1925   1950   1975

1870s George M. Wheeler leads Western Geographical Survey

1909 Admiral Peary arrives at North Pole

1911 Roald Amundsen reaches the South Pole

1926 Admiral Byrd flies over North Pole

1927 Charles Lindbergh flies across Atlantic

1937 Amelia Earhart disappears over South Pacific

1943 Jacques Cousteau invents modern scuba diving

1953 Edmund Hilary and Tenzing Norgay climb Mount Everest

1960 Jacques Piccard & Don Walsh reach the deepest point on earth in a submersible

1969 Neil Armstrong walks on moon

Bad Omen

Looks like a broken tea cup.

Spotted Coyote looked south. Something had startled a covey of quail in the draw. He motioned for silence. Even the small children stood as still as rocks.

He and a few other Shoshoni had come to hunt the Valley of Smokes once more before winter. But now something was coming. There was alarm when a hunting party of Utes emerged from the scrub oak. Spotted Coyote gripped his flint axe tightly. One of the Utes calmed his companions, then spoke to the Shoshoni. The old Ute only wanted to talk. Everyone relaxed. Spotted Coyote got his peace pipe and the men settled into a circle. The old Ute spoke slowly and was easy to understand, but what he said made no sense. Tribes in the south told of men with white skins who rode on dogs as big as buffalo. These men had magical weapons that could strike a man dead by pointing at him. The Indians talked long and late. One of Spotted Coyote's children wandered into the circle. As the pipe was passed, the child playfully grabbed it and threw it to the ground. Spotted Coyote and others gasped—surely this was a bad omen. But the old Ute only chuckled and brought out his own pipe. "You can't expect to keep nice things with children around," he said.

Shoshoni peace pipe
The Indians of Utah made pipes from stone, bone, rock, and clay. The pipe stem was wild rose, elder, or a hollow reed. Wild tobacco (kinnikinnik) and the inner bark of the red willow were ceremonially smoked.(Dotted line represents decomposed pipe stem.)

actual size

Map: Tribes
Indian homelands before white settlement.

Shoshoni

Gosiute

Ute

Paiute

Navajo

World News
1520–Aztec empire falls to Spanish under Cortez • 1522–Magellan's ships sail around the world • 1520s–30s Protestant Reformation in Europe • 1526–First English Bible • 1532–Inca empire falls to Spanish under Pizarro • 1535–Catholic monks work against exploitation of Indians • 1537–Pope issues *veri homines*, doctrinal statement that Indians are humans with souls • 1540–Francisco Vasquez de Coronado looks for fabled Seven Cities of Gold in American Southwest • Hernando de Alvarado arrives in Taos (present-day New Mexico) • Hernando de Soto encounters Indian Temple Mound culture in present-day Mississippi • Lopez de Cardenas discovers Grand Canyon • 1542–Coronado gives up search for Cities of Gold, returns to Mexico • 1542–African slave trade brought to the New World

History
The Utes, Gosiutes, Paiutes, and Shoshoni arrived in the area about 1300 A.D., possibly from the southwest. Though related and in some cases able to understand the other's language, relations between these groups could be hostile. The Shoshoni and Utes had frequent contact with the Plains Indians and adopted some of their ways. War parties raided neighboring tribes, with the Utes gaining an especially warlike reputation. The Salt Lake Valley was a buffer between the Utes, Gosiutes, and Shoshoni, who all used the valley for hunting game or gathering seasonal foods. Chance encounters like the one above certainly took place.

Tobacco had a ritual purpose among Utah Indians. Men began serious discussions by sharing a peace pipe. They believed the rising smoke carried their prayers to the heavens.

| 1500 | | | 1550 | | | 1600 | | 1650 | | | 1700 | | 17 |

N A T 1492 Columbus discovers New World • 1520 Cortez conquers Aztec Empire • 1533 Francisco Pizarro conquers Peru • 1590 English colony of Roanoke disappears • 1607 Jamestown colonized; Pocahontas saves Englishman John Smith • 1620 Pilgrims land on Plymouth Rock • 1683 William Penn signs treaty of peace with Indians • 1742 Peruvian Indians revolt against Spain **V**

Indian Paintbrush

Part of the snapdragon family, the Indian paintbrush is one of Utah's most beautiful wildflowers. Indians used it to make a black dye for buckskins.

Cattail

The cattail was an important source of food and material for Utah's Indians for thousands of years. Indians ate the roots and lower stem, wove mats with the leaves, and used the "fluff" for insulation.

Believe it or don't!

■ The Indian population of Utah before white settlement is a matter of guesswork, but a figure of 40,000 is sometimes cited.
■ The Shoshoni peoples of Utah are related to the Aztecs.
■ The Navajo came to the Southwest deserts from Canada 500 years ago.
■ The advanced Anasazi Indian culture of southern Utah suddenly disappeared 700 years ago, probably due to drought.
■ The region of the Great Salt Lake was virtually abandoned for a thousand years beginning in 500 B.C.

Lake Level

In 1540, the lake level was probably low, as the area was experiencing a 500-year drought.

UTAH BY THE NUMBERS

Estimated number of Anasazi archeological sites in Southern Utah: 100,000

In a studied burial site, percent of Anasazi women who died between ages of 16 and 26: 80

Percent of Anasazi men from same site who died before the age of 26: 60

Average life expectancy in eleventh-century England: 35 years

Maximum penalty for robbing archeological sites on public lands: $100,000 or 5 years

Utah Population: About 40,000.

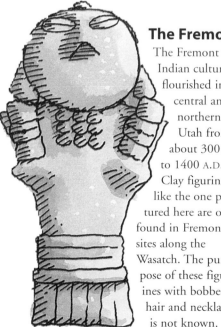

The Fremont

The Fremont Indian culture flourished in central and northern Utah from about 300 B.C. to 1400 A.D. Clay figurines like the one pictured here are often found in Fremont sites along the Wasatch. The purpose of these figurines with bobbed hair and necklaces is not known.

Pine Nuts

The Shoshoni, Utes, Paiutes, and Gosiutes differed from earlier groups in that they relied heavily on pine nuts, which are found in higher elevations, for food.

Wild Corn

Corn, or Indian maize, was developed centuries ago from wild corn. Improved varieties quickly spread between Indian cultures before the arrival of Europeans.

Chief Black Hawk

When Pioneers moved into Indian lands, conflict was inevitable. In 1865 a Ute named Black Hawk led a hit-and-run campaign against Mormon settlers. Between 50 and 70 people from each side died in the conflict before Black Hawk is reported to have asked for peace in 1868, saying, "I am sick of blood." As a boy, Black Hawk saw the first Utah Mormon-Indian fight at Battle Creek.

| 50 | 1800 | 1850 | 1900 | 1950 | 2000 |

1754 French and Indian War
1763 Chief Pontiac leads uprising against British
1811 William Henry Harrison defeats Indians at Tippecanoe
1814 Andrew Jackson defeats Creek Indians
1838 Trail of Tears—Eastern American Indians forced to the far West
1853 Utah Walker War
1863 Bear River Massacre
1865 Black Hawk War
1876 Sitting Bull wipes out 7th Cavalry at Little Bighorn
1890 Wounded Knee
1923 Indian-White dispute in Southern Utah leads to Posey War
1924 Congress grants Indians U.S. citizenship
1942 U.S. Army employs Navajos as code talkers
1990 7,273 people in Colorado, New Mexico, and Utah claim Ute ancestry

The Mammoth Hunters

Wow! An arrowhead!

The great beast grazed in a marshy stretch of shore. Ulat explained to Omokt that this was good—the mud would slow the beast. This was Omokt's first beast-hunt. He had proven his skills on rabbits and magpies, and now he'd been allowed to join the men. He was in awe of clan-brother Ulat, who knew so much about the great beast and made new and wonderful spear points. Omokt had one.

At the appointed signal they rushed the great beast with spears and atlatls poised. Omokt's thrust went awry and he found himself gazing stupidly at a broken shaft. Someone, Ulat maybe, screamed a warning. Too late! Omokt felt himself tossed high and then fall, fall, fall. The icy waters took his breath and he struggled against the shock and wet clothing. Just when he'd given up to join the ancestors, strong hands dragged him to light and air.

It was clan-brother Ulat. Not far away the others were already discussing ways to butcher the great beast, who still struggled weakly. Ulat called to them. "Look at the strange bird I found—it flies gracefully but swims like a rock!" The others laughed and Ulat gave him a rough hug. He felt foolish. But that night they gave him the prime piece of beast.

Map: Lake Bonneville 12,500 B.C.

Great Salt Lake

Salt Lake City

Utah Lake

Clovis Projectile Point
These distinctly American stone spear points first appeared 11,500 years ago.

actual size

World News 10,000 B.C.

Ice Age coming to an end; climate radically changes the ecology • People begin farming in Africa, Asia, and Europe • Britain settled as ice retreats • Clovis projectile points used in America • The bow and arrow invented • Mammoths disappear from Europe • The famous Lascaux cave paintings in France completed

Mammuthus columbi 11 ft. high at the shoulder

Paleolithic hunter with atlatl

History

About 12,000 years ago (10,000 B.C.) the last Ice Age was coming to an end. It was still cold and wet, but the glaciers in Utah's mountain canyons had begun to recede. Lake Bonneville, down from its high in 12,500 B.C., was still immense but rapidly shrinking.

It's impossible to know when humans first entered Utah. The earliest evidence is from 9,500 B.C. of people we call Paleo-Indians who lived by hunting and gathering. But it's possible the first people to set eyes on Utah's mountains and valleys were Ice Age hunters following mammoth herds who passed through leaving little trace of having been here.

10,000 B.C.	9000 B.C.	8000 B.C.	7000 B.C.	6000 B.C.	5000 B.C.
End of the Ice Age	North and South America widely settled	Earliest evidence of man in Utah / Mammoths extinct	Crops cultivated	Cattle domesticated / Sea levels rise as glaciers melt	Corn becomes important American crop

S T O N E A

Lake Level

Lake Bonneville at the Provo shoreline (12,500 to 10,000 B.C.) was about 4,700 feet above sea level. At the Bonneville shoreline (20,000 to 12,500 B.C.) the lake was about 5,100 feet above sea level.

Glacier Lily

Found in the canyons of the Wasatch, it blooms at the edge of snowfields in the spring

Bonneville Cutthroat

Thousands of years ago the Bonneville cutthroat trout may have grown to 30 lbs, about the size of a German shepherd. When Lake Bonneville began to shrink, the Bonneville Cutthroat retreated into streams of the Deep Creek Mountains in Utah's West Desert. It now commonly tips the scales at two or three pounds.

UTAH BY THE NUMBERS

Average temperature in Utah during Ice Age: 16° F cooler

Age of oldest juniper tree in Utah: 4,000 years

Percent of Utah's megafauna (large mammals) extinct by end of the Ice Age: 70

Average depth of Lake Bonneville: 1,000 ft

Average depth of the Great Salt Lake today: 10 ft

Square miles covered by the Great Salt Lake : 1,700

Square miles covered by Lake Bonneville: 23,000

Times the Great Salt Lake has completely evaporated in the last 8,000 years: 2

Believe it or don't!

■ Mammoth remains have been found throughout Utah—in Salt Lake City, Ogden, Tremonton, Sandy, Orem, Provo, Park City, and Canyonlands.

■ In 12,500 B.C. Lake Bonneville broke through Red Rock Pass and 1,000 cubic miles of water poured out in a matter of weeks. It created catastrophic floods throughout present-day Idaho, Washington, and Oregon.

■ The Huntington Mammoth was found in 1988 at an elevation of 9,000 feet—the highest mammoth remains ever found. It was a 60 year-old male who died about 11,300 years ago. Replicas of the skeleton are on display at the Fairview Museum and at the Utah Museum of Natural History.

Missing!

These large mammals, called megafauna, are missing and presumed extinct. They were last seen hanging around Lake Bonneville at the end of the Ice Age. If you should happen to see one, please notify your local paleontologist.

American Camel

Giant Ground Sloth

Arctodus (short-faced bear)

Mastodon

Saber-toothed Cat

Bison and Dire Wolf

Petroglyph found near Moab, Utah

| 4000 B.C. | 3000 B.C. | 2000 B.C. | 1000 B.C. | 1 A.D. | A.D. 1000 | A.D. 2000 |

Horses domesticated — Written language invented in Sumer — Rise of Egyptian culture and pyramids — Trojan War — Crusades

STONE AGE — BRONZE — IRON AGE — MIDDLE AGES — MODERN ERA

"Hey...Mom's calling..."

"Won't she be surprised when she
sees all this neat stuff!"

History

Utah in the early Cretaceous was hotter, lower, wetter, and buggier than it is today. Eastern Utah was a floodplain with sluggish rivers that drained from the Cordilleran Mountains in the west to a shallow sea that was beginning to split the North American continent. The shallow sea to the east kept the climate temperate, meaning there was little seasonal variation in temperature. Subtropical ferns, palms, redwoods, and cycads laid down thick mats of vegetation which, over millions of years, turned into the coal deposits now mined in eastern Utah.

Flowering plants were poised to sweep the world. Evolving right along with stamens and petals was an animal which would help make this botanical conquest possible—the honeybee.

Torrential flooding had eaten away huge chunks of riverbank. In the shadow of an especially tall embankment the dinosaur with the killing claws stalked her prey. The sauropod she eyed was huge, but obviously troubled by a painful forefoot. The sauropod paused and closed its eyes in weariness. The raptor struck like a loaded spring.

Digging into the sauropod's flesh with her forelimbs, the raptor slashed with the rear claws that were cocked like deadly scythes. But her victim twisted with surprising speed and the raptor tumbled to the ground. In a flash the huntress was on her feet ready to attack, but the sauropod surprised her again. Too late she saw the massive tail whipping around that sent her sprawling into the embankment. The eroded embankment gave way, burying the killer huntress in tons of mud and clay.

The sauropod nervously spun left and right, sweeping the scene for his attacker. She had disappeared.

Map: Museums and fossil sites

Weber State Museum of Natural History
● **Ogden**

● **Salt Lake City**
Utah Museum of Natural History

Provo
BYU Earth Science Museum

Dinosaur National Monument
Vernal ●
Utah Field House of Natural History and Dinosaur Gardens

● **Price**
Prehistoric Museum
Cleveland Lloyd Dinosaur Quarry

● Trilobite beds

Castle Dale
Museum of the San Rafael

Moab potash
Dinosaur tracks
● **Moab**

Escalante
Petrified forest

Blanding ●
Dinosaur Museum

Utahraptor
(20' long, 1,000 lbs.)

1/24th actual size

World in the early Cretaceous

World News 125,000,000 B.C.

Dinosaurs still 60 million years from extinction • Continental drift detaches India from Antarctica and sends it crashing into Asia—birth of the Himalayas • Flowering plants and bees arrive on the scene

225 million

TRIASSIC

Utah covered by shallow sea

Southern Utah covered by sand dunes

195 million

Birds evolve from dinosaurs

JURASSIC

Dinosaurs from Dinosaur National Monument washed up on sandbar and buried

136 million

Utahraptors run rampant throughout Utah

A G E   O F   D I N O

State Fossil
The Allosaurus roamed Utah in the late Jurassic. It is the official state fossil.

Allosaurus fragilis
140 million years

UTAH BY THE NUMBERS

Year first dinosaur bones were found in Utah: 1859

Tons of bone and rock removed from Dinosaur National Monument quarry: 350

Tons of dinosaur bones stored beneath BYU football stadium: 250

Number of different kinds of dinosaurs found in Utah so far: 35

Percent of dinosaur-loving kids who named Utahraptor as their favorite dinosaur: 20

Age of the oldest rocks in Utah: 2.5 billion years

Age of the youngest rocks in Utah: 5,000 years

Believe it or don't!

■ Moviemaker Steven Spielberg dreamed up the Utahraptor even before one was discovered. Early in the production of *Jurassic Park,* Mr. Spielberg decided the film's villains, a pair of 6 ft.150 lbs. velociraptors, were just too small. He insisted they be beefed up. The result was 20 foot "raptors" tipping the scales at half a ton. Concerns about authenticity were put to rest when Utahraptor was found a month later near Moab.

■ "Raptor" dinosaurs are close cousins of modern birds.

■ Coal miners in Utah often come across dinosaur tracks and bones preserved in coal deposits.

■ Dinosaur National Monument was established in 1915 near Vernal. It is the richest dinosaur quarry in the world.

Tempskya Fern
Found in eastern Utah coal deposits, this fern from 125 million years ago grew to ten feet.

Famous Utahns of the Past

Stegosaurus
140 million years

Parasaurolophus
65 million years

Diplodocus
140 million years

Brachiosaurus
140 million years

Uintatherium
"Uinta Beast"
48 million years

65 million

2.5 million

CRETACEOUS			TERTIARY		QUAT.
Coal beds formed in eastern Utah	Dinosaurs die out	Uintah Mountain Range formed	Volcanoes in western Utah	Granite used to construct Salt Lake Temple formed in Little Cottonwood Canyon	**Rise of man**

Triceratops
65 million years

S A U R S   AGE OF MAMMALS

UTAH BY THE NUMBERS

Depth of Lake Bonneville: 1,000 feet

Depth of the Great Salt Lake today: 10 feet

Number of people who lived in the Salt Lake Valley in 1849: 8,000

Number of "Forty-Niners" who passed through the Salt Lake Valley in 1849: 15,000

Year of first airplane flight in Utah: 1910

Depth of the Kennicott copper mine: One-half mile

Utah in square miles: 85,000

Utah's highest point: Kings Peak, 13,528 feet

Utah's lowest point: Beaverdam Creek, 2,000 feet above sea level

Record low temperature in Utah: -69° Fahrenheit in 1985

Record high temperature in Utah: 117° Fahrenheit in 1985

Number of polygamists who went to prison in the 1900s: 1,200

Number of Hispanics living in Utah: 90,000

Number of Asians living in Utah: 35,000

Number of African-Americans living in Utah: 13,000

Of every ten Utahns, number who are Mormons: 7

Median age in Utah: 26

Cancer rate in Utah: Half the national average

Number of people in the Mormon Tabernacle Choir: 325

Rank of Utah's population among the fifty states: 35th

Fine for not wearing a mask in Provo during the 1918 influenza epidemic: $50

Annual average temperature in the Uinta Mountains: 32° Farenheit

Annual average temperature in southwestern Utah: 61° Farenheit

Annual precipitation in the Great Salt Lake Desert: 5 inches

Annual precipitation in the Wasatch Mountains: 40 inches

Number of plant species in Utah: 4,000

Percent of Utah that is forested: 28%

People per square mile: 20

Number of students in public schools: 500,000

Number of students attending private schools: 11,000

Number of stone arches in Arches National Park: 1,500

Age of bristlecone pine trees in Bryce Canyon: 4,000 years

❖

Designed by Richard Erickson and Pat Bagley. Printed and bound in the United States.

10 9 8 7 6 5 4 3 2 1

Library of Congress Catologing-in-Publication data
Bagley, Will. This is the place / by Will Bagley.
p.   cm.
Summary: Presents information about different aspects of Utah's history as a sister and brother unearth various artifacts in their mother's garden.
ISBN 1-885628-25-0 (Softcover)   ISBN 1-885628-26-9 (Hardcover)
1. Utah–History–Juvenile literature.   [1. Utah–History.]
I. Title.
F826.3.B28 1995   95-40502
979.2--dc20   CIP